The Progressive Darkness

*For the Christian Losing
Hope in Depression*

Carl Binger, LMHC

WESTBOW
PRESS®
A DIVISION OF THOMAS NELSON
& ZONDERVAN

WestBow Press books may be ordered through booksellers or by contacting:

WestBow Press
A Division of Thomas Nelson & Zondervan
1663 Liberty Drive
Bloomington, IN 47403
www.westbowpress.com
844-714-3454

Scripture quotations are from the ESV® Bible (The Holy Bible, English
Standard Version®), copyright © 2001 by Crossway, a publishing ministry
of Good News Publishers. Used by permission. All rights reserved.

ISBN: 978-1-6642-2487-2 (sc)
ISBN: 978-1-6642-2488-9 (e)

Library of Congress Control Number: 2021903606

Print information available on the last page.

WestBow Press rev. date: 03/02/2021

"You don't hear people talk about these things much, especially in the Christian world. I think you are going to connect with a lot of people in ways they have not known as you bring these types of feelings and battles to light. I also think it's good you are sharing a positive experience with medication - how the journey out of the deep depression involved Jesus and medicine. Again, not something usually promoted as good and necessary in these circles, so I appreciated that and your balanced approach to not rush to that as the answer, but sometimes it is part of the solution."

-Melissa VanHeukelum

"Even though I wish you never had to experience the darkness that you have, I really appreciated you sharing so openly about your experiences and how God has used them to redeem them for good."

-Yahan Xie

"Carl does a wonderful job of walking the reader through his battle and eventual mental health victory. His honest account of struggling with depression and faith is descriptive enough that I think many people, particularly men, struggling would feel like they're not alone."

-Dr. LaRonda Starling

"Overall, this was really great. I felt so understood, and like we've known each other for quite some time. I think people will really feel connected and not alone. You really show how God was working through this dark time in your life, and how He was there with you while you even when you didn't "feel" His presence. So glad for the work of God in your life brother. This was a blessing for sure, and I know it will be for so many others."

-Dan Forte

"Carl, I am confident someone will read this book and feel a great sense of relief and like they are seen for the first time. What an incredible gift you are giving to people by sharing your story - and sharing the real struggle in detailed moments. Congratulations on creating a powerful work. I am moved and I am so excited for those it will help."

-Monica DiCristina

"If I had to use one word to sum it up, I'd say "hope". Your story conveys hope to the reader. And not like a surface-level, well-wisher type of hope. It's like someone reminding you that, even if you feel like you're floating off into the dark abyss, you're still tethered to the Anchor."

-Angela Berardi

"I'm enjoying what I have read thus far. Your honesty in sharing your story and your feelings throughout your journey is amazing. It's something I don't remember reading in other writing that approaches the topic of depression. It's real and raw and very refreshing in that you talk about this tension and wrestling with your mental health while still being a believer. The church doesn't deal with the issue in such a real way."

-Kevin Wilson

"Carl's story is a testament to his vocational aim: walking alongside those who are struggling where they are. Framed in personal reflection, The Progressive Darkness is told with an honesty that seeks to let in the Christian who is wrestling with depression and encourages hope via Jesus' style of ministry. Carl's inclusion of reflective poems adds another level of communication and resonate deeply. If you're looking for a voice to speak plainly about Christianity and depression, this book will be a welcome read."

-Abbey Sitterley

"It is often said that you can at once identify an expert by the ease with which he executes his craft or by the grace with which he distills high concepts such that the novice has a lively grasp of them. I am stunned at the ease of vulnerability that characterizes this book, and I cannot recommend it highly enough. Though its primary subject matter is the presence of clinical depression within the Christian community, the book is really a pithy primer for the church at large and should, in my estimation, be included in every church's library or resource center. It is a very raw and real look at that troubling intersection between the chemically-induced lies of depression and the true Christian's exhortation to "Examine yourselves, whether ye be in the faith' ...". This is not a theological text in the academic sense; rather, every line drips with practical insight into the mindset of one being ground in that agonizing and all too often unseen crucible. The book is raw, real, and effectual. It is not an exercise in navel-gazing, but its aim throughout is to point with intimate honesty to Jesus the Christ, the Sufferer of Sufferers, while gently but Biblically adjusting the lens through which the church has often and naively approached true depression. The title, The Progressive Darkness, is drawn from one of the Poems tucked away toward the back of the book. These MUST be read. They are pungent psalms of the soul, both aflicted and revived, testimonies in miniature of God's unfailing love toward His servant, even in his deepest sorrow. Really, there is nothing extraneous about this book; every word, from the Introduction through the Poems, Bibliography, and Further Reading, has been painstakingly culled but naturally presented, and one would do well to tease out line by line what Carl has so succinctly delivered in these few pages."

-Hwaen Ch'uqi

"Carl invites us into his heart and mind during the transformative faith journey of his life. Darkness certainly loses its power when you realize you are not there alone. Carl gives all who suffer with depression this gift and provides a personal, Christian perspective on our darkest seasons."

-Lindsay D'Alleva

"This book is a resource I wish I had during the time I was depressed. I believe it will help a Christians struggling with depression know that they are not alone, and that although well meaning people may disappoint or even hurt us in these times, we can find others who have walked a similar road and have our faith strengthened on the way. Ultimately, we will find that Jesus is the one who can best identify with us and heal."

-Josiah Klossner

"This book reflects the pain and despair that depression brings. It's a vulnerable account of an experience many people feel completely alone in. This book shines a light onto this dark topic and lets others know they do not have to suffer in silence. There is joy and there is hope in this book. There is the proclamation that mental health issues can happen to anyone, anywhere including those inside the church. And that treatment of those issues can include the church, professional help and medication, all at the same time. Carl, I appreciate your voice in normalizing mental health discussions and advocating for believers to get the support they need."

-Alaina Brubaker

To my lovely wife, Carissa, and my three dear sons,
Marcus, Derek, and Travis. Most importantly,
to my Lord and Savior Jesus Christ.

Contents

The longer you wait, the more emphatic the silence will become. There are no lights in the windows. It might be an empty house. Was it ever inhabited? It seemed so once. And that seeming was as strong as this.

—C. S. Lewis, *A Grief Observed*

I knew what the Lord was capable of. I have seen His great works of the past. I just needed a teaspoon of His grace for my wounded soul and I would be able to run around the earth for Him. This wasn't happening though.

I didn't know who I was any more. I just couldn't find my way to His door in the dark, no matter how hard I tried or begged Him to try. I felt my soul was dark and all I wanted was a spark. I just wanted some moments, even if they came every few days. The only thing that was really given me hope was in the midst of all of this hatred for God for putting in me this condition, I desperately wanted to be His child. I just wanted positive attention from my Lord. I wanted to know if He still loved me.

Foreword

In *The Four Loves,* C. S. Lewis brilliantly remarks, "Friendship is born at that moment when one man says to another: "What! You too? I thought that that no one but myself ...""

If you are battling through depression or love someone who is, reading *The Progressive Darkness* by Carl Binger will make you feel like you have discovered a new friend. Carl is unrelentingly transparent and authentic in the depiction of his own journey with depression. This is not a book with simple solutions or quick fixes. More than anything else, it is a look into the soul of a man who is inviting you into the darkest season of his life.

Ultimately Carl's story will also bring you hope. Depression did not define his life, and it doesn't have to characterize your life either. You will experience the freedom and joy that Carl discovers as he lets God and others into the deepest parts of his life.

I consider Carl Binger a friend. I trust that you will end up calling him a friend too as you journey with him through the pages of this book.

—John Iamaio

Acknowledgments

Thank you to the following:

- My sister, Felecia Drysdale, for helping to navigate the darkest time of my life
- Kimberly Cox, for creating the beautiful illustrations in this book
- Johanna Bond, for providing some edits and suggestions for my book

Thank you to all of the people who read over my draft and gave wonderful suggestions and encouragement: John Iamaio,

Mike Deskov, Kevin Wilson,

Rich Ortman, David York,

Gary and Mary Spitol,

Hwaen Ch'uqi,

Peter Englert, Dr. LaRonda Starling, Dan Forte, Dr. Dyona Augustin, Jardin Carlton, Patrick Penaherrera, Dr. Josie Augustin, Nathan Mancini, Monica DiChristina, Yahan Xie,

Melissa VanHeukelum,

Angela Berardi,

Abigail Sitterley,

Josiah Klossner,

Anthony and Lindsay D'Alleva,

and Alaina Brubaker

Introduction

As I reflect on my life, I believe the experience that affected me the most profoundly was my bout with depression. It was three years of pure hell. It started around August 2006 and ended somewhere around the end of the summer of 2009. Though three years may seem like a short time to some, every inch of it was hell for me. The depression started around the time that my brother got arrested and continued while I was a senior in college, wondering what my next career move would be. It was a time when the chemicals in my brain became unbalanced and the Lord was just allowing me to sit in the furnace for a while. Was I genetically predisposed to depression? Was it my diet or the stress from college?

As far as I can tell, several factors could have been a trigger to send me into that thick, deep darkness I endured. It could have been a mixture of some or all of these things. I can say with confidence that my experience of depression allowed me to know myself in much greater depth. It inspired me to be a counselor, to help those who are hurting mentally, emotionally, and spiritually. That time in my life, more than anything, helped me to trust more in the living Savior who raises the dead.

I wrote this book for many reasons. At the very heart of telling my experience of depression are my deep concern, care, and empathy for those who have suffered, or are suffering, a similar challenge. I recall what it was like to suffer almost completely alone in depression and to want help from God and Christians, feeling like I was getting it from the very least of these sources at times.

I pray by the grace of Jesus that this is a light of encouragement that can reach the dark corner you're in. I hope that those who are currently struggling with depression can read this book and come away with the thoughts and feelings that they are understood and valued and that God has not given up on them. In the following pages, you will find my account of the experience of depression from 2006 through 2009, some illustrations done by a wonderful artist, and a few poems I wrote recently as I reflected on that time of depression.

Before I talk about this dark time, I want to give a brief account of the brightest of times I had, when I came to faith in the living God, Jesus. Becoming a Christian was by far the most pivotal moment of my existence. It gave—and continues to give me—ultimate meaning. I truly hope this book is a blessing to you.

The Brilliant Light

From the summer of 2001 through the spring of 2003, I was attending Buffalo State College and studying urban planning. I use the word *studying* loosely because 90 percent of the time I was smoking weed and trying to find out where the next party was happening.

One night during my freshman year, I was sitting in my dorm room with my roommate and a young woman. All three of us were not even close to being practicing Christians. However, if pressed, we would all have probably professed some measure of faith in God. We heard a knock at the door. When we opened the door, another young woman came into the room with a look of excitement on her face. She had a piece of paper in her hand.

She said to all three of us that she had been on the internet and found something called "A Letter from Satan." She said it was a letter from Satan written to Christians who had backslidden or fallen away. After this announcement, she proceeded to read the letter out loud.

> *I saw you yesterday as you began your daily*
> *chores. You awoke without kneeling to pray. As*

a matter of fact, you didn't even bless your meals or pray before going to bed last night.

You are so unthankful; I like that about you. I cannot tell you how glad I am that you have not changed your way of living. Fool, you are mine.

Remember, you and I have been going steady for years, and I still don't love you yet. As a matter of fact, I hate you because I hate God. I am only using you to get even with God. He kicked me out of heaven, and I'm going to use you as long as possible to pay him back. You see, fool, God loves you, and He has great plans in store for you.

But you have yielded your life to me, and I'm going to make your life a living hell. That way, we'll be together twice in the fiercely burning fire of hell. This will really hurt God. Thanks to you, I'm really showing Him who is boss in your life, with all the good times we've had.

We've been watching dirty movies, masturbating, cursing people, stealing, lying, and being hypocritical, fornicating, and visiting dirty websites together. We've been overeating, telling dirty jokes, gossiping, being judgmental, backstabbing people, and disrespecting adults and those in leadership positions. We have bad attitudes and no respect for the church.

Surely, you don't want to give these all up. Come on, fool, let's burn together forever. I've got some really hot plans for us both here and in hell. This is just a letter of appreciation from me to you. I'd like to say "thanks" for letting me use you for most of your foolish life.

You are so gullible; I laugh at you. When you are tempted to sin, you give in. Ha ha ha! You make me sick. Sin is beginning to take its toll on your life. You look twenty years older, and now I need new blood.

So, go ahead and teach some children how to sin. All you have to do is smoke, get drunk or drink while underage, cheat, gamble, gossip, fornicate, and live, being as selfish as possible. Do all of these in the presence of children, and they will do it too. Kids are like that.

Well, fool, I have to let you go for now. I'll be back in a couple of seconds to tempt you again. If you were smart, you would run somewhere, confess your sins, and live for God with what little bit of life that you have left.

It's not my nature to warn anyone, but to be your age and still sinning, it's becoming a bit ridiculous. Don't get me wrong. I still hate you. It's just that you would make a better fool for Christ.

P.S. If you really love me, you won't share this letter with anyone.

Yours for as long as you want,
Lucifer

I had a strange feeling of guilt and conviction after she read the letter. I felt terrified, undone, and laid bare. I sensed in my heart that I was guilty as charged. I actually started weeping. The thought of treating God this way and siding with Satan somehow hurt me deeply. I could feel everyone's eyes on me as I cried. They seemed to be dumbfounded. I could tell they wondered why I was crying, but they didn't really say much.

After the two women left our room, my roommate said, "I can't believe you cried, dog."

I could only reply, "I don't know what happened."

I wasn't sure what just happened. It wouldn't be long until I knew why I felt the way I did, but for now, this was just a hiccup in my persistent time of rebelling against God. I went back to my ways of treating women poorly, using them for sex only, and deceiving them into thinking I cared for them. I continued smoking as much weed I could get my hands on in order to help pass the time in college.

During my sophomore year, my suite mates and I decided to pool some of our money together to buy weed to sell on campus. Long story short, we somehow got caught and were told not to return to campus for a week or two. If we did, we would be arrested on the spot. I can't tell you how awful I felt during this time. I had never gone to jail before, and it was looking like I would not only be expelled from college but I could also be facing jail time. I felt absolutely helpless and ashamed.

I didn't tell any family members, and I certainly would never tell my mother. I think I cried one night, and I know for sure I pleaded with God to rescue me from this situation.

I didn't really know for certain who He was, but I pleaded for Him to deliver me. I think He might have heard me.

When I returned to campus for the hearing, I was completely released from any punishment because no drugs were found directly in the room I lived in and I denied knowing about any drugs. It was as though nothing had happened, except I missed a week or two of classes.

I looked up to the sky and said, "Thank You, God, for getting me out of this."

I was thankful for a moment, but I soon went back to partying and doing me. I thought that if God were kind enough to release me from any punishment at school, He must have been okay with the way I was living.

Several other things happened that year. I recall thinking and talking about different incidents that happened in American history, such as the JFK assassination in 1963 and the Panama Riots of 1964. I even remember someone saying to me that there was a tape circulating on campus that involved the president and a terrorist shaking hands and conspiring together. All this did was make me fear the unknown and even influence me to start to fear my own government. Even a few fraternities on campus were showing documentaries on how the United States was treating other countries poorly.

Nevertheless, as terrifying as it was, it made me want to know more, and so I dove deeply into conspiracy theories. I thought to myself, *I can't even protect the people I love. How can there be a God if there is so much evil in the world?*

I thought some time shortly after that, *there must be a God, and if there is, He will judge evil.* The next thought shook me to my very core, *if there is a God, then He will judge me too!*

Within a couple months, it seemed as though I was aligned in God's crosshairs. He seemed to be firing rapidly at

His target, hitting me just weeks apart. I talked to and spent time with a female student whom I somewhat liked. I felt she was really starting to like me too, but I didn't really want to be in a relationship with her. In fact, I was mostly using her for sex. I didn't want to be tied down with a woman, and at that time, I thought it was cool not to be.

I walked this woman to her room late at night, and she asked me, "Do you want to be more than friends or just friends?"

I thought for a second. I already knew the answer. So, I said, "Just friends."

As I watched her, she let her head fall down slowly, and I believe I could see some tears welling up in her eyes as she walked away. I think we might have said goodnight to each other. I started to walk away, back to my dorm, about a mile in the other direction. I thought, *God will judge you for all the women you have hurt in this way.*

I felt like this was another sobering moment. What was going on? Why did I keep feeling these connections with God all of a sudden? These were not pleasant experiences at all. What was happening?

Not too long after this incident, I got on AOL Instant Messenger first thing in the morning, as was routine. I would wake up, smoke weed (if it were available), and check AOL to see who was online. As the news window popped up, a headline being displayed bothered me. It said something along the lines of, "Is Jesus Christ Coming Back for His Church During This Century?"

I thought, *I know for sure that I am not a part of His church.* Then I felt sad about this fact and wondered if it could be possible for someone like me to be a part of something like that, to be amongst God's people someday. This question sent me searching for answers.

It was now the late winter to early spring of 2003. My sister, Felecia, as far as I knew, was the only Christian in my immediate family. She lived in Rochester, New York, and would send me money all the time while I was in school in Buffalo. She was very kind to me. I couldn't have asked for a better sister. I knew she went to church, and all these recent events had me wondering if I should reach out to her.

So I did. I didn't do my normal thing, which was to call her and ask for money (so I could then go buy weed), but I called her and I asked if she had a Bible I could read. She seemed beyond thrilled about my inquiry and offered to pay for a brand-new Bible and have it shipped to my dorm. When it arrived, I didn't know where to start.

I believe she told me I should start with the Gospels. So I did. I didn't know what to expect. I had read and heard Bible passages as a child and figured it would be the same dry, boring stuff I heard growing up. It was different though; in fact, it was life-altering. I read about this man Jesus and realized, *Wow, He is nothing like the world makes Him out to be. He is so loving, kind, and powerful. Who is this Man?*

One statement I came across in scripture would start me on the path of further examining my very existence as a creature, His creature. In John 3, Jesus was talking to Nicodemus, and He said to him that in order for one to enter into the kingdom of God, he had to be "born of water and the Spirit". To be exact, Jesus stated, "Truly, truly, I say to you, unless one is born of water and the Spirit, he cannot enter the kingdom of God." (John 3:5 ESV). Instantly the image of water came to my mind. I thought of the properties of water and how clear—how clean—it was.

I thought about my own life: how selfish I was, how much I despised God and women, and how I loved to please myself by smoking weed and cigars and drinking alcohol.

I thought about what it really meant to know God and how absolutely pure He must be. I knew it was absolutely impossible for me to make myself pure like water, so the only thing I could think to do was keep reading in the scripture to see if Jesus presented any solution on how to be clean in this manner.

The more I read, the more the word became sweet to read. I mean it was literally sweet like honey to my soul to read the words of Jesus. It put me in absolute ecstasy to reflect on His words. I couldn't contain it in my heart. I had to talk about it. I started writing scriptures on little Post-It notes and pasting them all over my side of the room and all over the bathroom inside my suite.

One of my suite mates asked, "What? Are you a preacher now?"

I didn't think so. I just thought I had to share this sweetness with everyone.

These beautiful words from the pages of scripture stuck with me throughout the day. Then something occurred to me, "There are a lot of religions out there. How can I know that this is the one?"

I continued to wonder about this as I was leaving my dorm to walk to the student union to grab a bite to eat. I ran into a friend, Ron. Ron was in a Latino fraternity, and I had seen him many times on campus before. In fact, Ron was one of the fellows who invited me to watch the documentary on U.S. scandals across the globe. Historically, the Latinos on campus seemed to primarily stick to themselves, so when Ron approached me, I thought it was a bit odd. He asked me what I was doing that day and if I wanted to come by his place with a couple of people to read the word.

I didn't exactly know what the word was. I thought the word was another name for the Quran. I knew I wanted to know what the true religion was, so I agreed to meet Ron and his friends. Later that night, I found out they would be reading the same Bible I had been beginning to explore. This seemed to me to be confirmation from God that I was on the right path. We were all on the path to truth, and it seemed as if we had finally found it together, outside of the fear of conspiracy theories.

The more I read the scriptures, the more I slowly started feeling the need to cut some behaviors out of my life. I was starting to feel that it was wrong to sleep around and treat women like dirt. I even started thinking, *maybe it wouldn't be so bad to be married someday.* Getting drunk was starting to feel a bit overrated. I continued to smoke weed until I went to visit my sister in Rochester one weekend.

After spending a Saturday at her apartment, the plan was to go to church with her the next day. As I sat up in my bed that night, I could only think of what was going on in my life during this brief time of exploration with God, particularly with Jesus's statements in scripture. I said to Him, "God, I know that I myself have been doing drugs, but I just don't know if I can stop on my own. I want to surrender this habit of smoking weed to You and surrender my life as well."

I laid down and went to sleep, but when I looked back in my journal, I saw that I prayed that prayer on or around April 20, 2003, which is National Weed Smoking Day (an official holiday for potheads). I thought that was amazing or cool what God did with the "4 20" thing.

Over time I gradually cut ties with most of my non-Christian friends. It's not that I didn't love them anymore. I just couldn't go on doing the things I used to do. It was hard not doing those things and still continuing to maintain a friendly relationship. A lot of people thought I went crazy.

I started being nice to women, and I stopped smoking weed completely. Friends would offer me weed all the time, but I would just say, "No thanks." I actually started paying attention in class, something I hadn't done in my two years in school. Because of potential negative influences from my old friends, I knew I had to spend more time with Christians, and so I moved to Rochester, where my sister lived.

It was June 2004. I had been living in Rochester for over a year now. I had become a member of my sister's church and had been baptized. While working at a community center, I heard about a summer job opportunity of a lifetime. In fact, my boss at the time was strongly urging me to apply for it. It was a job working in the beautiful forest of the Catskill Mountains. It was rent free with meals provided, and I would be teaching twelve- to fourteen-year-old kids lessons about ecology. This was special to me because I remembered flying to Moose River, Maine, as a thirteen-year-old and enjoying all the wonderful beauty of nature there.

I remembered how life-changing it was to be in the beauty of God's creation, and not wanting to miss out on this opportunity, I applied and actually got the job. I spent my first month out in the Catskills. While on this job, I experienced one of the longest and highest mountaintop experiences with Jesus. I sensed an overwhelming spiritual nearness to Him. I enjoyed what seemed to be one-to-one walks with the living Christ.

His presence seemed to be so absolute in my life, and as a result, my understanding of my final destination after my death became pretty clear in my heart and mind; it would be with this astounding person. Surely the Catskills was an easy place to see the Maker's handiwork, and so it was natural that He would make Himself known there.

Every glance at nature reminded me of how wonderful He was, and every provision for me displayed His loving care. It was as though I was in heaven already, except I couldn't see Him. During those days, it was so easy to pray and listen to Him. A mountaintop experience indeed it was. It would be a few years before things took a turn for the worse.

Dim

It was around August 2006. It was my first semester of my senior year at the College at Brockport. It wasn't a typical start of the semester of coming out of a summer and going into a fall of fun, football, and wings. Instead the world slowed down. My mind became dim. The intrigue I once held for the historic buildings on campus began to darken like ebony. I noticed that the long walks I took between classes to look upon the beauty of the trees no longer seemed to impress or refresh either. The glorious feeling of joy over simple things seemed to fall away into jet-blackness.

If that weren't enough, I began having heart issues. I wasn't sure if it were acid reflux, stress, or health issues resulting from consuming energy drinks. I went to a gaming place with my friends, Arena 51, and we'd go every once in a while, and pay around six dollars an hour to play on these really fancy computers. I would buy at least one really strong energy drink that had a warning label on it to not consume more than two types of this drink within a week. As far as I could recall, my diet was not great either. I would eat out at the college cafeteria and have all types of fattening foods during the week and on weekends.

The days dragged. I started to lose interest in things I

once enjoyed. I had a lot of books on theology that I studied habitually, some very expensive that waited patiently for me to read them. Over a few months, I found myself giving them away at literally no cost to the lucky recipients.

Why in the world did I feel like I was in a funk? As I continued to fight these feelings of disinterest in possessions, hobbies, and even Jesus, I tried my best to find comfort in how Jesus delivered me from some of my past sinful behaviors. I reflected on situations in which I almost got arrested on a few occasions or when I almost got a few women pregnant while living wildly during my senior year in high school. I found myself taking courage in and often finding a measure of encouragement in knowing that Jesus really saved me from some really bad moments from my past.

The power and reality of these memories seemed to lose their power over the next few months. It was like I was slowly falling into an unseen abyss. I tried to take some comfort in the fact that there were some Christians I knew who were having similar feelings around their faith and mental health. This too helped for a short time but lost most of its power as I continued the descent. To where, I don't know. I do know it was absolutely horrifying at every new turn.

To this day, one of the most miraculous things to me, aside from the Lord preserving me from walking away from the faith, was the fact that I didn't turn to drugs during this agonizing time. I had vowed that I would never smoke weed again since the day I became a believer and was delivered from it on April 20, 2003. I thought if I went back to it, it would be one of the surest signs that I had committed the unpardonable sin. No one but Jesus could have given me the grace to not go back to this drug, which was very much addicting to me. I even tried to reflect on this, but it too soon lost its strength. It's almost as if God were stripping me of every comfort. He was laying me bare. But why? I didn't do anything as far as I knew.

There were moments of joy and clarity still. At one time, my friend, Dave, who lived in Buffalo, like me, was going through darkness himself. One day, Dave and another person we knew from school were visiting Dave's apartment. Our friend was dealing with similar symptoms of darkness as well, so we decided that we would read the letter of 1 John a couple times through. This letter focuses on assurance for the Christian, which we so desperately yearned for, that God loved us still.

After taking turns reading a chapter, a piece, out loud, we made it through the epistle at least two to three times before stopping. All of us reported a noticeable difference in our mood and disposition toward Jesus. Though it only lasted a few hours, I recall it being a blessed and joyful break in the darkness that was slowly taking over. As the days and weeks followed, Dave and I would talk over the phone.

One thing he encouraged me to do was to seek after the Lord hard when I had moments of clarity, like we had at his apartment while reading the scripture. It wasn't that I was not seeking God otherwise. I was. It's just that the moments of clarity made it so much easier to do so. When I didn't have the feeling that darkness was breathing down my very neck, everything became easier. However, these moments of clarity, or spiritual highs, were becoming few and far between. It made me cherish these moments when they came around, and it made what was once common to me feel indescribably and noticeably different from every fiber of my being because I was being denied these blessings.

A cold sweat and shortness of breath awakened me one night. Sprinting to the bathroom, I splashed cold water on my face and begged God for mercy as I had an imminent feeling of death. Was I having a heart attack? What was wrong with me? I had been staying at my friend Dave's apartment. My friend, Pat, and I were visiting from out of town. Pat slept soundly before I woke him up to inform him of my experience and the need for me to drive back to Rochester to get checked out. On the drive back to Rochester, Pat encouraged me to focus on the goodness of God in scripture. I tried. It was terribly hard to see it.

Back in Rochester, I received two different heart exams and was told my heart was perfectly fine. This didn't bring much relief as I was convinced something was really wrong. I was taking Pepcid AC and drinking red wine to soothe this problem over time, which did seem to help a bit.

I would later find out that these were symptoms associated with depression, anxiety, and stress. I continued to have this physical and mental adversity. I was still dumbfounded by what was going on as I couldn't pinpoint why I would be going through such a thing.

My thoughts and feelings had become my greatest foe, and I was surprised that even people I trusted seemed opposed to me. When I expressed my concerns to a potential girlfriend, she told me quite matter-of-factly that I needed to get over whatever I was feeling and to just "suck it up."

To add insult to injury, a close friend commented, "Man, you're still going through that?" The most painful blow came from one of my best friends, whom, upon hearing of mine and some other Christians' struggles with depression, suggested that this feeling of depression must be "the great falling away" that Christ spoke of in the New Testament. Was this what God thought of me?

"Just suck it up, Carl! You're still going through this? You have fallen away!"

As you could imagine, this was very painful to hear from friends. These were people I knew were Christians but sinners just like me. To say that they didn't understand what I was going through would be the most catastrophic understatement. Their very words confirmed to me what I had already been feeling deeply, that I didn't belong to God, especially never had and never would. Their words were on par with my equally slanderous thoughts. It was impressive how something that seemed like a simple statement absolutely dismantled my person.

Given any other situation, these words wouldn't have been that bad; however, in this darkness of depression, it seemed my dark thoughts were now taking the form of my very friends around me. It was manifesting and no longer in my head. I would've rather been wounded by an enemy or an acquaintance, but please, God, not my friends too! I would have preferred a stabbing than these words from friends. I lost God, my friends, and joy.

What was the reason for living at this point? What was next? Was there anything else to lose? Could it get any worse? It felt like I was receiving a Devine stiff arm of sorts. I wasn't actively rebelling against God in a way that I was aware of. So why did it seem He hated me and was targeting me? I could manage to walk through a day or two in this darkness of depression if sunshine were promised the next day. However, weeks, months, and years under this condition seemed insidious, and I felt confident it would slowly break down the mind, body, and spirit. There were some moments of hope as I dragged through my final year in college.

I was able to have a sliver of joy and assurance during a philosophy class. In this class on that day, the professor brought up that there was a resurrection spoken of regarding Jesus Christ.

One student smugly said, "We don't even know if that happened."

As sad as I was at that time, I felt a fury burn in my soul against the other student for uttering those words. This brought me great comfort as I thought, *I must love Jesus still if I am getting angry when people dismiss His claims. Maybe, just maybe, the Holy Spirit is real in me still. Maybe I still have life in me.*

I journaled and savored the moment. I started to feel that maybe if I had a change of scenery, I would feel better.

You're Here But You're Not

Ebony

During spring break from college, I went to visit a good friend, Jay, a native of Rochester, New York. He had recently moved from Rochester to Florida. The smell of Florida is so distinct. The scent, the vegetation, the palm trees, the grass, and the air is simply beautiful. It was home after all. I was born in Florida and lived about the first four years of my life outside of Orlando before moving to western New York.

I wondered, *Could I ever live in a place like this as an adult?* At times it seemed like the very garden of God and home. Other times, it seemed so worldly and glitzy. And giving the state I was in, Florida presented an opportunity to pursue all manner of sin.

But as lovely as Florida was, I still felt empty while there. I knew I should have been having fun, but I wasn't. The depression was robbing me of every ounce of enjoyment. There were moments where I felt like God was with me, like things were normal again, but most times He felt distant. In this state, I couldn't get a firm grasp on whether or not God was my friend anymore. I felt He was there when favorable things would happen, like me losing my wallet at the movie theater and then finding it shortly after. I could even feel the accompanying joy and real gratitude of recovering my possession.

There was another instance where I remembered waking up early and going out on my friend's balcony to read the account where Jesus raised Lazarus from the dead. Jesus gave me real peace as I read the account, and I found myself just praying, "God, this is all I want, to feel alive again. Please don't give me over to these dark feelings again."

Then there were the times in Florida when the joy was just gone. Later in the day after the great balcony devotion, sitting next to a beautiful pool and hot tub didn't yield pleasant feelings. The darkness crept in again. A day or two later, going to Universal Studios for a nice walk in the cool Florida air seemed like it could help. Jay and I would be linking up with another great friend, Pat. We would have a drink or two and spend time in one of the nightclubs. *Maybe this would help*, I thought, but instead it was like twisting a dagger in a wound.

I distinctly thought as I looked around the club at the people dancing and the musicians playing, *Man, if I only had an ounce of joy that everyone else has, I would be able to enjoy the moment*. The sense of normal wasn't coming.

As my visit was winding down in Florida, I think Jay could perceive that I wasn't the same as he had remembered when he lived back in Rochester, and he said, "I miss the old Carl who was on fire for Jesus."

That didn't help matters much. It made me feel more depressed. I couldn't seem to change it. In fact, I could not change the way I felt. I was at the complete mercy of God and this cloud I was under. Wrapping up the night, I listened to worship music, hoping to lift my mood. Forcefully I even sang along at times. I prayed with Jay. Nothing happened.

There was what felt like a mounting offensive to abandon God within my heart.

I kept thinking, if God truly loved me, He would come after me if I left. I didn't want to leave, but I felt my hand was being forced. These urges became even stronger when I saw non-Christians seeming to have more joy and fun than I did. What was the point of living for God anymore if I loved Him and He didn't seem to love me back?

After I returned home from Florida, the darkness progressively grew as I finished college. I had dark thoughts and feelings more and more frequently. Keep in mind that while I firmly believed I was dealing with a spiritual depression, I had no idea there was such a thing as clinical depression, or at least I didn't think I had it. I firmly believed that God was just disciplining me and I was just going through a dark time, like most saints in the Bible, and had to faithfully just wait until He brought me out on the other side.

Though I had some moments of hope in Florida, a change in scenery and a break from things didn't seem to help much. I got to thinking maybe the change in scenery wasn't long enough. Perhaps I needed to be around some brothers in the faith whom I knew really well, the same brothers I was around when I first came to the faith while attending a previous college in Buffalo. A couple of them had moved to Delaware with their families, so it seemed like a logical landing spot after graduating. Therefore, around the middle of August 2007, I decided to make the move to Delaware.

Falling into the Abyss

Jet

While I was in Delaware, I was staying with my good friend, his wife, and their little son. There were some early signs of God's favor in the form of me having two interviews lined up almost immediately upon getting to Delaware. One job prospect was as a tutor at the University of Delaware, while the other was an assistant manager at a YMCA summer camp. I ended up taking a third, and later option, as a TA at a small alternative high school. This was a very small school of about twenty students, but make no mistake, the work was brutal for me.

I was tasked with occasionally performing multiple restraints on teenagers who had learning delays and behavioral challenges. I should have been thankful, right? I had a job fresh out of college, I had multiple job offers and interviews, and I was with my friends whom I loved more than just about anyone. Who wouldn't be happy?

Let me tell you, it was humanly impossible to hold on to the blessings of God in this state. If a person who struggles with anger sees red, as a person who struggled with depression, all I saw was black. And as if adjusting to a new place and added stress from a high-stress job wasn't enough, my sleep started to become disturbed. This had to be one of the most brutal stretches of depression for me. It lasted the length of time I was in Delaware, from the middle of August to about the middle of September.

I was starting to sleep a couple hours per night, waking up so often that it felt like I was awake every five minutes. I would go into work unbelievably drained the next day to face the stressors of a student acting out. Even on calm days, I just felt so worthless and felt like dying. I dreaded my very existence.

There were close to zero positive feelings about anything in life at this point, and reading my Bible only brought me more dread and seemed to confirm that I was no longer a child in God's kingdom. Every positive scripture I read assuredly was for some other Christian, but every scripture of judgment was tailor-made for me. I felt my mind saying, *Just get high and drunk. You should start sleeping around again. This Jesus thing is a hoax. It was good while it lasted.*

My friends around me tried to encourage me in the faith, but it felt absolutely useless. I didn't believe their words. I wanted to. I even entertained the thought that they were lying to me just to help me feel better. I thought that they believed deep down that I really was a reprobate. I was around people but felt absolutely abandoned while constantly questioning if God loved me anymore. Oh, the existential loneliness of it all. I wouldn't wish it upon anyone.

A beacon of hope came in the form of some email exchanges I had with a friend back in Rochester. She was a Christian and also dealing with severe depression. I was somewhat delighted that I wasn't alone in the world and that maybe, just maybe, I could still be a child of God and be dealing with depression at the same time. This delight would only come in very small waves. With every positive sign and tiny victory, there came a massive blow to me mentally, physically, spiritually, and emotionally. I can recall inviting friends from Rochester to visit me and even asking my mom to consider moving down. I was desperate and had no idea what to do. While I didn't have a plan to kill myself, I did have thoughts of dying.

In Delaware, I drove a '95 SAAB. It was starting to emit smoke from the hood of the car each time I stopped at a red light. Under normal circumstances, I would have cared enough to get the car repaired, but now I didn't care if the car exploded with me in it. The feelings of dread increased. My constant companion was a Sith lord.

If I had a mustard seed of hope at all, it was dashed by the oddest of dreams I had one night. In the dream, I was an observer in a parking ramp at night. I saw a big brawl happening between a group of black and white men. There was nothing particularly sexual about the dream; however, I woke up from the dream with a nocturnal emission. I thought that was weird as this type of dream would never have caused my body to respond this way in the past. In fact, I can't ever recall having had a dream like this ever.

As I sat in bed confused by it all, I would start an even darker path of depression. How could this be possible? Why did my body respond this way to this dream? Well, the thought that came next was a vicious accusation about my sexuality. My mind said, *You are gay.* I tried fighting this accusation with logic by bringing up my track record of interest in only women. My mind insisted, *You are gay.*

I thought to myself, *It was just a dumb dream with no sexual themes at all. How in the world can being gay be a conclusion that I arrive at?*

It was as if my mind were deciding for me and against me saying, "Even if you don't have a record of being interested in men, why would you have the dream about men fighting and then have a nocturnal emission? You usually only have those when you dream of women, right? However, you had this happen when you were dreaming of men. And though you weren't sexually aroused, the body doesn't lie."

I reasoned, "Well, I don't know. I can't control my dreams."

My mind continued, "Well, deep down inside you must be gay because your body responded a certain way."

No matter what logic I tried to use, my mind was relentless. It was a nonstop accusation. It was an assault on my mind like I have never felt before. It was absolute mental abuse by what seemed like an invisible force. It was malicious and insidious. It didn't seem to rest until I was destroyed.

After this night, the next morning the thoughts would return. It didn't matter what activity I was doing or how hard I tried to think of something else. I kept getting the thought, *You are gay.* I still found women extremely attractive and had no intention of being gay, but my thoughts kept saying, *You're gay,* almost as if to force me to be gay.

I found myself exhausted from trying to fight these thoughts. I knew I wasn't gay. There was no evidence that I was even remotely gay except for this accusatory thought that followed this odd dream and my body's response to it. At times I felt my mind was cracking in half. My brain was fried from all the rumination. I was physically, mentally, and spiritually tired.

I began to think, *I don't know. I must be gay because my*

mind is saying I am gay. Oh no, now I really am a reprobate. God has given me over to reprobation.[1]

My mind agreed, "He sure has. I told you He doesn't care for you. He never has and never will. You are doomed." It was a nonstop battle against the scathing accusations of, "You are not God's child" and now "You are gay."

I couldn't take it anymore. I had to move home to Rochester. Over the next few days, I talked to my boss about having to resign from my job. My boss was amazing. He was very understanding when I approached him. I told him how rough things had been for me and that I needed to put in my two weeks' notice. He seemed to be a bit disappointed that I was leaving as he thought I was a great fit for the job, but he agreed that it was probably best for me. As time went on that day, the depression seemed to get the best of me, and I found myself urgently needing to talk to my boss again. This was unbearable. I needed to do something.

I went back to my boss and said, "Hey, you know what? I'm sorry, but I need to leave in a week instead of two weeks."

Again, my boss was understanding. He was even understanding when I came back again at the end of the day, in tears, saying I couldn't wait for even a week and I had to leave that day. It was the end of the workday, and I

---

[1] As a side note I would like to say, if a professing Christian is struggling with homosexual thoughts and actions, I am not saying they are a reprobate. What I said of myself above was how I was processing things at the time. My thoughts and feelings were communicating to me that (1) if I was having these thoughts then I must be gay and (2) now God is making me sink further and further away from Him because I wasn't previously gay, and now, was apparently so. On the other side of depression, I came to know these thoughts as irrational thoughts related to the depression I was going through.

was standing outside with four of my male coworkers crying like it was nobody's business. I just didn't care anymore. I couldn't care less if these men thought I was weak or not man enough. I should have felt the Lord's compassion at this moment, but all I could feel was darkness.

One of my coworkers spoke up and told me about how he once left his hometown to work someplace far and became really homesick at one point too.

My boss said to me, "Carl, here is a hundred dollars. Drive straight home and don't stop. Call me when you get home."

I didn't drive home right away. I went back to my friend's house where I was staying. I packed my things and left the next morning. My friends asked me to reconsider. I couldn't. I think somewhere in my mind I was pondering, *If I am going to die, it probably should be where my family is.*

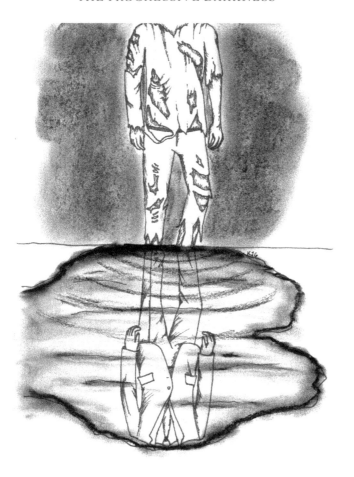

I Don't Even Know Who I Am Anymore

Vanta

On the drive home to Rochester from Delaware, I drove faster than I have ever driven in my life. I figured if I got home, my depression would somehow drop at least a bit. Being around family and what is familiar had to be a measure of tonic to these fatal soul wounds. Until this point in my life, I had never received a speeding ticket or been prone to speed.

Today was different though, for obvious reasons. As I was speeding through Pennsylvania, a state trooper pulled me over. You couldn't pay me to muster up a single care for the ticket I thought I was about to receive.

As the officer approached my vehicle, he asked, "Did you realize you were speeding?"

I replied, "Yes, sir. I am sorry. I am just trying to get home."

He looked at all the things packed in the back of the car. "Are you moving or something?"

"Yes, sir. I actually just graduated from school and moved to Delaware, but that didn't work out."

He said, "I am just going to give you a citation. Please watch your speed."

To be honest, I didn't care if the trooper gave me a ticket, arrested me, or shot me. Again, the depression wouldn't allow me to perceive this non-ticket as a merciful blessing from God. Instead, as I continued my drive, I began to curse God out loud because of the darkness. The darkest thoughts of God came to mind. The most hateful feelings stirred up in me toward Him. I thought to myself, *God, if You hate me so much, why don't You just kill me? I am already living in hell. Don't You plan on sending me there anyway?*

I arrived in Rochester later that night. Most of that trip was still a blur in my mind. Immediately upon my arrival in Rochester, I was able to obtain a job as a paraprofessional (a teaching assistant) and classroom float for a kindergarten class. Miraculously, my smoking car continued to hold up, even after driving it from Delaware to New York in under seven hours. To top it all off, the next morning my soul felt very much the complete opposite of the previous day of terror, so much so that I couldn't help but give God praise for it and think of the scripture passage, "Weeping may tarry for the night, but joy comes with the morning." (Psalm 30:5 ESV)

Again, I tried holding on to these blessings, especially when feelings of joy and belonging accompanied them. I wrote these thanksgivings in my journal and meditated on the events over and over while also reflecting on scripture passages. Holding on to these precious moments was the very definition of grasping for straws or trying to hold water. It was impossible. It felt like God was toying with me and I could soon expect the rug to be pulled from under me with breakneck speed.

Knowing that these moments were becoming far more infrequent was also killing me on every level. What a cruel game for the Master to play on His servant, or the Father His child, assuming I was that.

While back in Rochester, I would often reflect back on my friend, Dave, whom I lived with in Delaware. I remembered how he had gone through a brief period of depression while he lived in Buffalo. By this time though, he was no longer depressed. It seemed God had spared him while passing me over, and this caused resentment to rise in my heart. I was overlooking all the great things my friend and Christian brother had done for me during these dark times, just as I had been doing with God.

So when I moved back to Rochester, I wrote him an email expressing my frustration with how I was still suffering and how God was essentially wrong in sparing him and not me. Upon reflecting on it, it really was a pitiful email, but such was the sad state of my soul.

The moments of darkness were really progressive. In the beginning, it started off as a few days a week of this dreadfulness. Months in now, and it was every day. When joy came, it was exceptionally powerful. I got into the habit of running on the treadmill as I heard that exercise could boost my mood. In addition to this, I changed my diet, took a milk bath, did yoga, and took St. John's wort, whatever it took.

In the midst of all these efforts, I headed down to the basement of my sister's house where I was staying, and as I reached the bottom of the stairs, I felt an indescribable peace. I fell to my knees in tears and thankfulness that the Lord had suddenly broken the darkness in just a moment in time. I was in disbelief. I thanked God and begged Him, "Please don't leave me to the state of depression again." The darkness would, however, return again later that day.

At one point, someone suggested I visit a Christian counselor. I visited this man, whom I highly respect very much to this day. He gave me much helpful insight into my depression. He loved Jesus deeply and was a student of the Bible. He was very encouraging, and every time I met with him, I felt my soul being ministered to. He would always encourage me to sing to the Lord and ask questions like, "If you truly were a reprobate, why do you care so much about being one?"

My only hope now was that my very desire to be accepted by God was proof enough that He loved me and was working in me. My counselor echoed the words previously spoken to me by a woman who was walking away from the faith a year before. This woman said, "You must be one of the elect; otherwise you wouldn't care so much."

The only problem I had with my counseling brother's advice was that he seemed to be strongly opposed to any treatment that included medication, the same impression I got from most Christians when this topic of treatment came up. Most seemed to be saying that I should read scripture, stay in fellowship, pray, repent, and sing to the Lord.

None of these means of grace put any dents in the darkness I felt. In fact, I grew angry that other Christians seemed to be enjoying the Lord and not me. I became even more frustrated because I couldn't pinpoint a blatant sin that I was committing and of which I was not repenting. I just couldn't understand why a loving being like Jesus would have me suffer so much while providing fewer and fewer intervals of relief for me. Why would He surround me with so many people who didn't seem to fully understand my plight?

Months after these appointments, I recall the morning where I clearly wanted to die the most. I had really reached the end. This was the day I am convinced that, had I not gotten help, it would have resulted in the path of me planning to kill myself. Before the depression, I used to gain great joy from working with children. I had worked with them most of my life up to this point. But now, no smile or laughter of children could make me the slightest bit happy. No pain of a child could draw any empathy from me. Now, there was no measure of gratitude in my journal that could curb this darkness. The light was completely gone. It had mostly been almost gone, but now it was completely gone.

I felt death in my heart as I poured my morning coffee. I didn't know how I planned on killing myself, but I was tired of fighting. It's not that I desired suicide with a sick type of joy. I simply wanted to escape the hell of the existence I was living in. It did not concern me how anyone felt about me anymore. It was all about me and how to end this pain that no one seemed to be able to fix. In essence, it seemed like I failed myself, along with everyone else, including God. I didn't even care about hell on the other side. I just wanted to die. The thought of loathing the sight of a child was enough to know I was coming to the end of my life.

I was in the kitchen that morning getting ready to go into work when my sister must have seen death in my face, which reflected perfectly what was in my heart.

She said, "Carl, it's time that you get help."

For far too long, what other Christians had said about medication held me back. My own thoughts held me back too. I thought if I took medication, it would prove many things, like I really wasn't a man, my faith had really failed, and I really was weak, crazy, and an utter failure. I had fought taking medications for too long though. It was now time.

A very small part of me was holding out hope that maybe medications would help; however, I mostly thought nothing would work. If seeking God by His means didn't work, how could a man-made means work? If the medications didn't help, I thought I would end up being back at this suicidal moment in short order. So I made an appointment to see a psychiatrist, and shortly thereafter, I was prescribed two medications to help with mood and sleep.

If I recall correctly, I felt the immediate positive effects of the medication. I absolutely was not at 100 percent, but I definitely noticed a difference. Two things changed almost immediately, if not shortly, after starting the medication. First, I slept much better, and second, the constant accusation of being gay melted away. So there was still a journey ahead of me, but it was so much more manageable compared to the two years of hell I had just crawled through.

Somehow I got my hands on some old sermons from Charles Spurgeon, who famously suffered from depression. I looked up and printed every sermon remotely related to spiritual depression while continuing to exercise, eat well, take my medications, and seek God's face in His word. Slowly things changed. I wouldn't have pitch-black days but I would just have moments where I thought, *Man, I feel better, but God is still missing.* I continued, *If He is not here with me, what is the point of feeling better?* I needed and wanted God's blessed assurance that He was with me, no matter what.

As 2008 rolled around, there was an uptick in positive moods and experiences. In 2008, the Giants beat the Patriots in the Super Bowl. This was a peculiar situation because even as a Bills fan, I found myself extremely happy that the Giants won the game in such a stunning fashion. I was jumping up and down at my sister's house while letting out roaring cheers. This type of positive emotion had been absent for a very long time. I was able to feel again. I was shocked by it all really. Maybe there was hope of recovering from this after all.

The summer of 2008 was a very pivotal turn for the better regarding the depression. That summer, I worked for the second time in my career with the New York State Department of Environment Conservation as a camp counselor at the summer education camp.

Here I worked with teens and preteens aged twelve to fourteen. I taught ecology lessons while also engaging in rec, hiking, canoeing, fishing, and tent camping. For me, next to if not higher than journaling, being outdoors is one of the best ways to connect with God. Obviously reading scripture, prayer, and being around other Christians should be of the utmost priority for a believer. However, supplementing these means of grace with journaling and being outdoors adds a certain luster to the Christian life. Being out in the wilderness is nothing short of seeing the handiwork of God on display. With this and the many things I listed previously, over time, I felt better and better. For me, by God's grace, these things were certainly polishing my soul into a gleam that I had once thought was impossible to experience again.

After all was said and done, could I proclaim that Jesus was and is good to me? In a word, absolutely. Digging deeper, outside of the negative thoughts and feelings associated with depression, I'd be hard-pressed to find anything to point to the contrary. What came from such an awful time period for me? What did God teach me, and what did I learn?

Let Me Out of This Gloom

Return of the Light

So what did I learn as I went through this great trial? It has definitely been the greatest one in my life, at least up until this point. I learned that suffering is never a reason to sin but an opportunity to serve and be served. I learned that music is very powerful medicine. I learned the immense value of sleep and how God has blessed us with this dear gift. Sleep is an irreplaceable tonic, and I must steward the great gift of sleep well as to function at my peak emotionally, spiritually, and physically.

I learned that my feelings do not reflect my faith. No matter what I feel, no matter how good or bad I feel, this has no bearing on my standing with God. If my feelings were an indicator of my salvation, I would be saved and unsaved every day.

I learned that my depression could have been linked to many factors, including poor diet, lack of exercise, stressors of college and uncertain career options, genetic predisposition, being pruned by God, and being tempted by Satan.

I learned true vulnerability. Man fails to be vulnerable, but Christ has done so and perfectly. Man sees vulnerability as a weakness. Christ sees it as true strength and the essence of being a human that He created in His Father's image.

How else can we pray for one another and be healed if we are not vulnerable and confessing our sins, weaknesses, and struggles to one another (James 5:16)?

Although Christ never sinned, He did display his weakness through His humility, telling his friends of his inward pain while requesting their assistance to pray with Him (Mark 14:34). These truths, coupled with the experience of depression, helped me to become more open and honest about my feelings, sin, and suffering. In short, I learned that a perfectly vulnerable Christ can make a perfectly sinful man vulnerable, even more so than ever.

I learned that my love deepened for Christ. I cherished more deeply the cost of His suffering as the God-Man. Oh, how Jesus must have loved us to come suffer in the way He did! No matter what happens to me in this life, I, nor anyone else, can suffer more than what Christ has ever suffered during his life and on the cross. After recovering from depression, I realized biblically and experientially that the God I was dealing with was the same God who knew suffering, sadness, and darkness more than anyone ever could. This was the Jesus I was dealing with and not some mad God-King, although my feelings said differently throughout most of my depression experience.

I learned that though God's love is extreme, His judgment is also severe. Jesus was not exaggerating when talking about how awful hell is. So what happens when God is mad? It made me contemplate what the emotional condition would be of those who finally and completely reject a Christ as Savior whose love is so deep. At least in its current state, it's called a place where the "worm never dies," a place of "weeping and gnashing of teeth," and "outer darkness." This biblical imagery paints nothing short of an awfully dark and depressing existence apart from God.

I learned that even though I was suffering, it enabled me to serve in ways I never thought of before. Depression allowed me to feel like a sorrowful man; it allowed me to taste some of what this hurting world is feeling collectively and be activated by God and my own suffering to serve those who hurt. I could better identify with the Man of Sorrows, Jesus, although I only felt His closeness sporadically during the time of depression. In addition, I learned through my serving in depression that it compared nothing to how Jesus poured Himself out to service to others. I was simply given grace to imitate my master during these trying times, and this was a great privilege.

I learned that just because medications eventually worked for me didn't mean that it would help others in the same way. I also learned that there could be two extremes that people could jump to when depressed: run to medications almost immediately without doing any spiritual self-examination or completely block out all forms of treatment and just read and pray away their depression.

I've learned that prayerfully pulling from both arenas can be the most helpful. Contrary to popular beliefs within the church, I strongly believe Christians can be faithful to God while taking medications. No Christian would question a cancer patient prayerfully taking chemo, so why question a patient who is taking a medication that will help them mentally? Also consider that while God is more than capable of healing anyone, He has blessed many people with gifts to help His creatures as well, doctors and counselors being some of those helpers.

I learned that some of the greatest signs that depression is taking hold of you include the lack of enjoyment of most things you used to enjoy, changes in diet and sleep, and thoughts of suicide and/or dying. Depression is not having a few bad days. It is not something you can "just suck it up" or "man up" about. Struggling with depression does not mean God hates you; in fact, this could be an occasion where God has drawn close to you or at least given the opportunity for you to call on Him to do so. He wants us to draw closer to Him even when our feelings encourage otherwise.

I learned that unless one really sits down and really observes someone with depression, specifically their actions and their words, one can be completely oblivious to the depression that one is staring in the face. While I was in Florida with Jay and we met up with Pat at Universal Studios, Pat would later tell me he had no idea I was depressed during that time.

I learned that depression is everywhere in scripture; it just uses different language like sadness, troubled in spirit, darkness, and so forth. I love pointing to the most central character and blessed figure, Jesus Christ. Just a few instances in Jesus's ministry that mention some form of depression and despair include John 11:33, Isaiah 53:3, Matthew 26:38, and John 12:27. There are also instances of such around people like Jonah, Job, Elijah, David, and Paul, to name a few. On top of this, another crucial thing I learned from reading passages like these and many others were that just because you are depressed, it does not mean you have lost your faith. God is close to the humble and brokenhearted more often than not.

I learned that the world being plagued by such a darkness as depression really should not come as a shock to me, considering that we live in a fallen world where our physical bodies fail us frequently. That being the case, is there any wonder that our mental faculties fall with such catastrophe? What a joy it will be in heaven to not only have fully functioning and perfected bodies but also fully functioning and completed perfected neurons in our brains. I am thankful to Jesus for medical doctors and researchers who can provide aid to the ill mind in the form of counseling, medications, exercise, good diet, or other means to help those who struggle with depression.

I learned to be thankful in all things, even in the awful darkness of depression. It is a command from God that kept me sane through most of it, and it was one of the last things that seemed to lose effectiveness against the darkness of depression. On top of this, I learned to treat every positive interaction, gift, and blessing in depression as coming directly from Jesus Himself. After all, He is the author of all good things and the one who cares infinitely more than even the most caring human could imagine (James 1:17).

As you can see, the Lord Jesus taught me plenty during this time. It was not in vain. If He did this for me, He will certainly do this for you. If all this weren't enough, the Lord blessed me to be able to help many people with similar struggles during and after my time of depression. I changed my whole career track from teaching/sociology in undergraduate to counseling in graduate school. I now actively seek the individuals suffering alone in silence, through counseling, writing, workshops, and other educational outlets. I moved on to eventually open my own private practice called Luminance Mental Health with the slogan, "being a light to depression."

If I could say something to one struggling with depression right now, what would I say? I would say this, "No matter what you feel, if there is any fight to hang on to Jesus, if there is any hatred for sin, if there a struggle within you against the dark that presses you constantly, then God is working in you, and you can take hope in that. Use that knowledge and keep running back to Jesus in scripture."

A passage in scripture that still encourages me immensely can be found in John 6:37(ESV). Here Jesus says, "All that the Father gives me will come to me, and whoever comes to me I will never cast out." In those dark times, this said to me that no matter what I was feeling or thinking, as long as I came to Jesus, pleading for His help, He would not ultimately cast me out. The hope is in the coming.

How many times do we see in scripture where Jesus invites people to come to Him over and over again? When we come to Him, we can rest assured that this is not a work of man—as we naturally hate God and run from Him—but a work of God who loves us dearly. So go to Christ and keep going. He loves you and will reveal it in some way at some point, and when He does, thank Him and praise Him for it.

Thank you for taking this journey with me. May God through His Son Jesus Christ be a continual source of blessing and light to you.

Poems

I put together the following poems well after my depression experience. I wrote these poems as I reflected on the depression of the past.

It Was a Great Run

It was a good run or, should I say, a crawl for me.
Some really underestimate the hurt that this curse can be.
It's like You have Your back to me
While also stabbing me.

I thought You were the faithful one, the one who healed the broken sons.
When You said "It is finished," I never thought, "I'm the finished one."

What happened to Your love for me? Will You ever come for me?
You said that if I came to You, You'd never let me free.
Yet it's a mystery how Jesus Christ has abandoned me.

Because of Your grace, I can say this race was a great run.
But what was the point if I didn't know the raised son?
Now I'm in terror; I feel my faith is the fake one.

Weak Faith

It's like every time I take a sip from the fountain,
I'm left pouting because my faith can't move any mountains.

My faith right now couldn't even move any excrement.
My sufferings are large, like multiplying by an exponent.

I'm so screwed; most days I curse You.
I feel imprisoned, and all my days are sanctioned with dark
curfews.

I'm a brown man, but my heart is black.
I'm a grown man, but I'm acting like a brat.
I've had panic attacks.
My mind is ready to crack.
I have no defense because I'm vexingly sad.

Was I genetically predisposed to be disposed?
My once lively faith has started to decompose.

I'm not happy often.
I'm down like a coffin.

Dark Waters

God seems pleased with making me weak in these dark waters.
Not only is it night, but I am in the shark quarters.

I'm exhausted like long flights, mixed in with shark bites.
I'd rather jump down two flights than face this next wave
of true fright.

My mind is turning like waves; I'm burning inside with all rage.
Before I head to my grave, I meet with endless caves.

These are unfixed depths,
Nowhere to place my steps.
This deep is cosmic; it's gaping.
Unplumbed and spacious,
It's gaping and yawning,
Where vicious life is spawning.

I'm in a losing battle, you see, throwing sand at Helm's Deep.
The deep is breaking my knees; I'm quickly drowning to sleep.

What Depression Is Like

It is the worst darkness imaginable; it's a dark tower that's tangible.
In severe form, it's completely unmanageable.

At best, it's a horror movie come to life.
At worst, it's a horror movie that lasts an eternal life.

It is a giant titan chasing me, a disease content with razing me,
A heavyweight boxer who's waited years to face me.

It's tall and thick, a velvety black curtain.
It's a God-awful tent, and death feels certain.

It's a room in the place of gloom, a room in hell.
I feel doom in this pit, and the walls just fell.

It's an existential loneliness, the far side of the moon.
Give me an exorcist for darkness; I'm so over this gloom.

It's somber, rayless, and dismal; it's caliginous.
It's smokey, moonless, and abysmal; it's atramentous.

It's a progressive—aggressive—darkness.
It's an "I'd pay every penny to be rid of" darkness.

It's lonely like Pluto or Voyager 1.
I can't imagine what these moments were for God's only Son.

If Depression Were a Person

If depression were a person, he'd eat your lunch food.
Then he'd punch you before putting you in his mouth to munch you.

It's being chased by Darth Maul,
Sheer terror in dark halls.

It would be closely related to Hitler, a nightmare framed picture,
A Vantablack fixture with zero light as mixture.

It's impenetrable shade, millions of graveyards he's made.
If it were a demon, he'd be the highest of ranks, carrying diamonds as blades.

This hunter will trace your steps and often take your breath.
There's no time to pace yourself, dealing with death itself.

Some think it's a game until it's chasing them.
Then they wonder why the wounded prefer chasing death.

Sunshine

You're my sunshine, and You loved me before time,
Way back like my hairline.

Thank You for this coruscation, a much-needed vacation.
My death was certain without your illumination.

Florida couldn't bring radiance; sex couldn't produce resplendence.
Depression was only broken by the king of Phosphorescence.

I thought I lost Your essence, but now I see You beckon.
There never was a point where You wouldn't have let me back in.

I will worship You, champ, because You burn like a lamp.
I know You love me even after this painful boot camp.

I can cry for years from this brilliant lucidity; I was convinced of lunacy.
I thought I would die, but You preserved me perfectly.

You're my sunlight, my moonlight; You only do right.
The black vibes are gone, and my face shines with blue light, Your true light.

You transformed all of the night.
I regained all of my sight; I worship with all of my might.

And though I don't always agree, I trust when You choose fights.
Though I don't always believe, praises pass through my windpipes.

Your dazzle motivated me to start my own business, Luminance.
You made the dark, causing a spark; I can't deny Your influence.

There's no chance of outdoing it; Satan wishes he could ruin it.
And though he steals, kills, and destroys, no destruction comes through to me.

I trust the Gardener, though it hurts when He's pruning things.
You're the tried and truest king; I fix my eyes on the truest bling.

With a rugged heart and my flawed reason,
Your melodies melt this man of treason.

You're the light in every season,
No matter if I see it.

Jesus Christ, Jesus Christ, You are holy,
And Your grace tastes sweeter than cannolis.

Yours is a sunshine grace matched with a sunshine face.
After this trial, I am more confident that You will help me finish the race.

Reader's Guide

The goal of this activity is to take one's eyes off self and despair and to place them squarely on Jesus Christ Himself. I hope you find this short activity inciteful and encouraging. I would encourage you to pray and read over the following account alone or in a group.

As you read, reflect on how wonderful and caring Jesus is not just in this account, but in other accounts of scripture. Could such a tender Lord really reject a bruised and wounded soul? I believe this following passage really highlights not only how Jesus is an empathetic High Priest but also a Wonderful Counselor! I truly believe in this passage we can see how Jesus was both, but especially the best counselor. We should all make it our effort as believers to be this compassionate to our brothers and sisters in the faith when they struggle in such a way of despair and lack of faith in Christ.

How Jesus Counseled

In a group or on your own, pray for wisdom and guidance before you start. Read the scripture passage out loud and then to yourself.

Luke 24:13–29

- **He was intentional about His care as He drew near to the men (15).** They didn't have to look for Him. He came after them much like He went after the lunatic and many others. While Jesus was and is the most approachable person there is, He will pursue His children.

- **He listened well (19–24).** Jesus let the men talk without cutting them off. He listened patiently, allowing the men to clearly voice their sadness, frustrations, and unbelief.
- **He encouraged with scripture (27).** The source of spiritual encouragement can only come from a spiritual source, which is God and His word. Jesus utilized this resource to help these troubled men.
- **He asked questions (17, 26).** Jesus employed this practice of asking questions throughout His entire ministry. As any good teacher or counselor does, He asks really good questions to get the student to think deeply.
- **He challenged them (25–26).** These men were very sad, but the sadness could have been somewhat alleviated had the two men thought about the truths related to Jesus's situation more appropriately.
- **He allowed for vulnerability (17).** Jesus didn't say, "Listen, chumps. You need to man up and stop being soft." Jesus provided a space for these men to be sad and, in due time, moved to encourage them.
- **He spent time with them (27, 29).** It must have taken a long time for Jesus to go through all those books of the Bible that He mentioned, but then on top of that, He went to their home when they asked Him to stay. At no time do you get the sense that Jesus was in a rush to go or did not value these men's time.

What are some additional thoughts you had during your time of study?

Resources

I read through the following books, some multiple times, during the dark season of depression. I hope you will take advantage of some of these great resources during your time of trial:

- *Surgeon's Sorrows* by Zack Eswine
- *Stand* by John Piper
- *Out of the Blues* by Wayne Mack
- *Dealing with Depression* by Sarah Collins and Jayne Haynes
- *Christians Get Depressed Too* by David Murray
- *When I Don't Desire God and the Hidden Smile of God* (two books) by John Piper
- *Seeing in the Dark* by Gary Kinnaman
- *Feelings and Faith* by Brian Borgman
- *Depression: A Stubborn Darkness* by Edward Welch
- *The Shadow of the Cross* by Walter J. Chantry
- *Life as a Vapor* by John Piper
- *Pierced by the Word* by John Piper
- *Tempted and Tried* by Russel D. Moore
- *Battling Unbelief* by John Piper
- *Spiritual Depression* by Martyn Lloyd Jones
- *Faith Tried and Triumphant* by Martyn Lloyd Jones
- *The Bruised Reed* by Richard Sibbs
- *A Lifting Up for the Downcast* by William Bridge
- *Night of Weeping Morning of Joy* by Horatius Bonar
- *The Doubting Believer* by Obadiah Sedgwick
- *Trouble of the Mind and the Disease of Melancholy* by Timothy Rogers

Bibliography

Ige, Temi. "A Letter From Satan." TakingITGlobal. https://www.tigweb.org/youth-media/panorama/article. html?ContentID=2189 (Accessed Januaray 18, 2021).

Lewis C.S., A Grief Observed (New York: HarperCollins Publishers, 1994), 6.

About the Author

Carl is a husband to Carissa and the father of Marcus, Derek, and Travis. He has been following Jesus since 2003 and has been practicing counseling since 2014. Carl enjoys connecting with people and hearing their stories. Carl hopes to spread a message of hope to everyone who struggles with depression. Carl has an unrelenting drive to increase awareness of depression while also breaking down the stigma associated with getting help. Carl continues this work by writing, conducting groups, facilitating educational workshops, counseling, and doing talks in the community. Carl is the owner of Luminance Mental Health Counseling and the founder of the Surviving Depression podcast and Facebook group. For more information on what Carl is doing and free resources, please visit his website at www. Luminancemhc.com or join the supportive Facebook group and listen to the podcast both named Surviving Depression.